BUSTED!

NATIONAL GEOGRAPHIC
KIDS

MYTHS

BUSTED!

JUST WHEN YOU THOUGHT YOU KNEW WHAT YOU KNEW . . .

By Emily Krieger
Illustrations by Tom Nick Cocotos

CITY SEWER SWIM CLUB

NATIONAL GEOGRAPHIC

WASHINGTON, D.C.

CONTENTS

THE AVERAGE PERSON SWALLOWS FOUR SPIDERS IN THEIR SLEEP A YEAR.

ORIGIN

The origin of this myth is a mystery, spider experts say. And beware the myth within the myth: A report that the idea appeared in the 1954 book *Insect Fact and Folklore* is false.

BUSTED!

THERE IS NO SCIENTIFIC STUDY ON HOW MANY SPIDERS PEOPLE SWALLOW IN A YEAR; THE NUMBER FOUR IS MADE UP.

Spider experts say it's highly unlikely that even one of our eight-legged friends would crawl into a person's mouth. And it's even more of a stretch that the spider would then be swallowed. So rest easy, and with your mouth open.

Though two types of creatures are commonly called "DADDY-LONGLEGS," only one is a true spider. The way to tell the difference: True daddy-longlegs spiders have a body divided into two sections, and all eight legs are attached to the front section.

9

8 MORE SPIDER MYTHS BUSTED!

ALL OF THE FOLLOWING STATEMENTS ARE UNTRUE. READ UP ON SPIDERS TO FIND OUT MORE!

1 SPIDERS ARE INSECTS.

2 MOST SPIDERS CAN'T BITE PEOPLE BECAUSE THEIR FANGS ARE TOO SMALL.

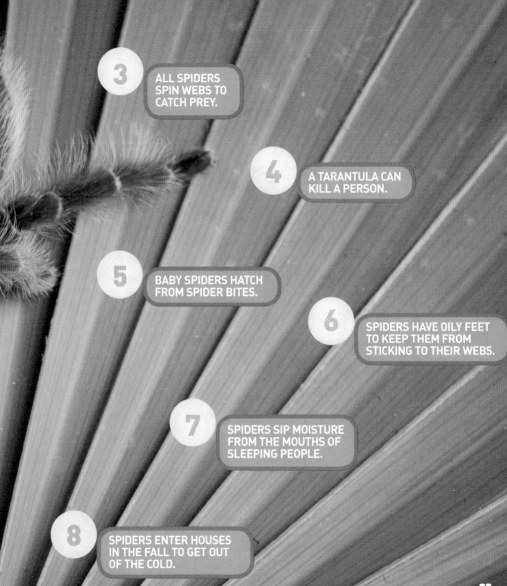

3 ALL SPIDERS SPIN WEBS TO CATCH PREY.

4 A TARANTULA CAN KILL A PERSON.

5 BABY SPIDERS HATCH FROM SPIDER BITES.

6 SPIDERS HAVE OILY FEET TO KEEP THEM FROM STICKING TO THEIR WEBS.

7 SPIDERS SIP MOISTURE FROM THE MOUTHS OF SLEEPING PEOPLE.

8 SPIDERS ENTER HOUSES IN THE FALL TO GET OUT OF THE COLD.

MYTH

EARTH'S ORBIT OR ITS ROTATION WOULD BE ALTERED IF EVERYONE JUMPED AT THE SAME TIME.

ORIGIN

With the planet's population at seven billion and counting, it's easy to think that all that people-power could affect Earth's motion.

BUSTED!

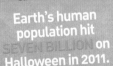

Earth's human population hit SEVEN BILLION on Halloween in 2011.

IT WOULD BE REALLY HARD TO GET EVERY PERSON ON THE PLANET TO JUMP IN UNISON. But it would be impossible for even such a giant jump to affect Earth's movement. The mass—the amount of matter, or bulk—of the human population is no match for the mass of the planet.

MYTH

PIGS ARE FILTHY.

ORIGIN
Yes, pigs wallow in the mud, so things can get messy.

16

BUSTED!

BEING MUDDY DOESN'T MEAN A PIG IS NOT CLEAN,

says Harry Snelson of the American Association of Swine Veterinarians. Long ago, pigs learned to use mud to meet their needs: It's a natural sunscreen, an insect repellant, and a way to keep cool. Pigs are so clean that they refuse to, um, "go" where they sleep.

Footballs are nicknamed PIGSKINS. In the old days, they were made in part from a pig's bladder (not the pig's actual skin).

MYTH

PORCUPINES THROW THEIR QUILLS.

ORIGIN

Threatened porcupines wag their quill-covered tails. This defensive move sometimes shakes loose older spines that can pierce nearby predators.

18

BUSTED!

PORCUPINES USE MUSCLES TO RAISE AND LOWER THEIR QUILLS. But they can't aim and shoot the spiny structures.

A threatened porcupine will also CHATTER ITS TEETH, turn around to show its rear, and run backward!

MYTH

POINSETTIAS,
THE POPULAR
CHRISTMAS
PLANT,
ARE
DEADLY
POISONOUS.

ORIGIN

A toxic tale that a toddler died after eating
the plant started to circulate in 1919.

BUSTED!

MANY STUDIES HAVE DETERMINED THAT POINSETTIAS AREN'T POISONOUS TO PEOPLE, and the plant's toxicity to pets has been greatly exaggerated. Research has shown that while the plant's milky sap can be a mild irritant, accidentally ingesting a few dozen or even hundreds of the leaves would at most cause a stomachache or vomiting.

The milky fluid in poinsettias is called **LATEX,** and it shares several compounds with the latex harvested from rubber trees to produce things like gloves and balloons.

MYTH

ONE DOG YEAR EQUALS SEVEN HUMAN YEARS.

ORIGIN

The myth's math is "overall, not that bad," says Washington State University (U.S.A.) biologist Kelly Cassidy. "The average dog does live to be around 10 years, plus or minus a couple of years. The average person lives to around 70."

BUSTED!

THERE IS NO ONE-SIZE-FITS-ALL CALCULATION BECAUSE NOT ALL BREEDS AGE ALIKE.

In general, heavier dogs have shorter life spans. Also, many dogs live into their early 20s, ages that in human years would make the pets at least two decades older than the oldest person. Bluey, considered by many to be the longest-living dog ever, died in 1939 at age 29—that's 203 in human years.

The longest-living person to date, France's Jeanne Louise Calment, lived to be 122 YEARS AND 164 DAYS OLD.

5 OF THE OLDEST-LIVING ANIMAL SPECIES

CLAMS

IN THE CHILLY WATERS OFF ICELAND LIE CLAMS NEARLY 400 YEARS OLD!

TORTOISES

HARRIET THE GIANT GALÁPAGOS TORTOISE LIVED TO THE RIPE OLD AGE OF 175.

FISH

ROUGHEYE ROCKFISH TOP OUT AT 205 YEARS OLD.

WHALES

SCIENTISTS WHO EXAMINED THE EYE OF A BOWHEAD WHALE ESTIMATED ITS AGE TO BE 211.

SEA URCHINS

A STUDY OF RED SEA URCHINS REVEALED THE SPINY CREATURES CAN LIVE FOR AT LEAST 200 YEARS.

29

MYTH

SCIENTISTS HAVE BROUGHT DINOSAURS BACK TO LIFE.

ORIGIN

The movie *Jurassic Park*, based on a popular science fiction novel, presented an exciting—though deadly—world where dinosaurs live alongside humans.

30

BUSTED!

The *Stegosaurus* and *Tyrannosaurus* NEVER BATTLED IT OUT—about 80 MILLION YEARS separated the dinosaurs.

SCIENTISTS HAVE REVIVED ANCIENT BACTERIA AND A 30,000-YEAR-OLD PLANT. But dinosaurs, which lived millions of years ago, are much more complex beings that even the most dedicated scientists aren't able to bring back to life—yet. But, stay tuned, they're working on it . . .

MYTH

WOMEN
TALK MORE
THAN MEN.

ORIGIN

Old proverbs from many cultures promote the idea that women are chattier than men. The book *The Female Brain* sparked a lot of conversation on the subject when it repeated the claim in 2006.

BUSTED!

The world's LONGEST LECTURE, given in Poland in 2009, lasted 121 hours—and was delivered by a MAN.

MANY SCIENTIFIC STUDIES HAVE FOUND THAT WOMEN *DO NOT* TALK MORE THAN MEN. For example, a 2007 study found that women and men speak about the same number of words per day—16,000. And that's all there is to say about that.

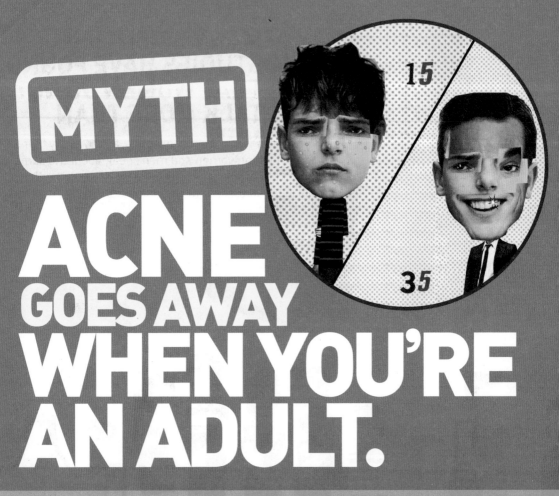

MYTH

ACNE GOES AWAY WHEN YOU'RE AN ADULT.

ORIGIN

Acne most often—but not exclusively—strikes teenagers.

BUSTED!

ADULTS GET ACNE TOO.

The blemishes happen when tiny openings in your skin called pores become blocked with oil. Skin is generally oiliest during adolescence. But a pimple can pop up at any time in life—even babies get acne.

The word *ZIT* first appeared in the English language in the 1960s as teenage SLANG FOR ACNE.

MYTH

FOOD DROPPED ON THE GROUND IS SAFE TO EAT WITHIN FIVE SECONDS OF BEING DROPPED.

ORIGIN

One legend claims that some 800 years ago, Mongol warrior-ruler Genghis Khan proclaimed food safe to eat after it had spent hours—not seconds—on the floor.

BUSTED!

IN 2003, AN ILLINOIS, U.S.A., HIGH SCHOOL STUDENT TESTED THIS MYTH FOR A SCIENCE PROJECT.

Cookies and gummy bears spent five seconds on a floor with harmful *E. coli* bacteria. When the teen looked at the treats under a microscope, she found that all of them had been contaminated with the germ.

A 2008 study by Swiss scientists found that the FLU VIRUS could live on paper money for up to three days. When MUCUS FROM A SNEEZE or cough also landed on the money, the virus could live as long as 17 days.

SURPRISE!
7 THINGS
DIRTIER
THAN YOUR
TOILET

KITCHEN SPONGE

CUTTING BOARD

BATHROOM COUNTER

44

KITCHEN SINK

BATHROOM FLOOR

KITCHEN FLOOR

BATHROOM SINK

MYTH

EGGS CAN BE BALANCED ON END DURING THE VERNAL EQUINOX.

ORIGIN

This kooky myth stems from science and traditional beliefs about the vernal equinox, the first day of spring. The season is associated with growth and birth, which the egg symbolizes. Also, daytime and nighttime are nearly equal, or balanced, on this day.

An omelet, a quiche, and a hardboiled walk into a pan...
What do you think? You're a STAND-UP comic now?!

BUSTED!

On April 1, 2007, 9,753 children searched for 501,000 EGGS in the world's LARGEST EASTER EGG HUNT, held in a Florida, U.S.A., theme park.

THE TRUTH IS, EGGS—OR BROOMS, ANOTHER MYTH—CAN BE BALANCED ANY DAY OF THE YEAR. Most people try to balance an egg for the first time on the vernal equinox, after hearing about the myth. When they pull off the feat, they assume it couldn't be done on any other day and therefore don't try it again.

IT'S BAD LUCK TO PICK UP A "TAILS-UP" PENNY.

ORIGIN

"Heads" and "tails" may have been thought to signify "beginnings" and "endings." That could be why heads (beginnings) is thought to be lucky, and tails (endings) isn't.

BUSTED!

PEOPLE PICK UP "TAILS-UP" PENNIES ALL THE TIME WITH NO PROBLEMS.

In fact, there's about a 50-50 chance of a coin landing that way. Calling "heads" or "tails" has been a tradition for centuries. Kids in ancient Rome even called "navia aut caput" (ship or head) because their coins had a ship on one side.

A PENNY DOUBLED EVERY DAY for 30 days is almost $11 million.

MYTH

IN *STAR WARS*, DARTH VADER SAYS, "LUKE, I AM YOUR FATHER."

Luke,
I am your
father.

ORIGIN

For decades, millions have uttered this famous quote—despite the fact that it contains one wrong word.

BUSTED!

THE LINE IS ACTUALLY "NO, I AM YOUR FATHER." In 1980's *The Empire Strikes Back*, Darth Vader delivers the shocking news to Luke Skywalker after a lightsaber battle.

In Disney's *Snow White and the Seven Dwarfs* movie, the Evil Queen doesn't say, "MIRROR, MIRROR ON THE WALL, who's the fairest of them all?" She says: "Magic mirror on the wall, who is the fairest one of all?"

55

MYTH

DUCK QUACKS DON'T ECHO.

ORIGIN

The tail end of a duck's quack—*aaaaaaaack!*—fades out, which can make it hard to hear the sound's echo. In addition, the bird's soft sound may not create an audible echo without the aid of nearby cliffs or other large structures.

BUSTED!

DUCK QUACKS DO INDEED ECHO.

In 2003, scientists at the University of Salford in England placed a duck named Daisy in a chamber and recorded her quacks—and echoes.

A TINY AQUATIC INSECT called a water boatman makes the world's loudest animal call for its body size. Though the bug is smaller than a grain of rice, its song, sung from the bottom of a river, can be heard by someone standing at the water's edge.

MYTH

A CHEMICAL IN POOL WATER WILL TURN YOUR URINE PURPLE.

ORIGIN

To keep pool water clean, and to protect swimmers' skin and eyes, a pool's chemicals must be checked regularly. One of the tests mixes a small sample of pool water in a container with clear drops that react, turning the water purplish. This tells the test taker what changes need to be made to the pool's chemicals.

BUSTED!

THE CHEMICAL THAT TURNS WATER PURPLE ONLY TESTS SMALL SAMPLES OF POOL WATER.

"The chemical isn't in the pool to begin with," says chemist Stephen Theberge of Merrimack College. As for an official urine detector? "It doesn't exist," says David Rouse of BioLab, Inc. No chemical, he says, will change urine's color without changing the rest of the water, too. In other words, the chemical would turn the whole pool purple!

Scientists in Singapore have developed a urine-powered battery.

63

MYTH

BATS ARE BLIND.

ORIGIN

Many kinds of bats have small eyes and don't rely primarily on sight for navigation or hunting.

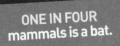

ONE IN FOUR
mammals is a bat.

66

BUSTED!

BATS AREN'T BLIND; ALL BATS CAN SEE.

Megabats—larger bats that include fruit bats—search for food using sight and smell. Micro-bats—which include the smaller, familiar snub-nosed bats—mainly hunt by echolocation. In this system for detecting movement and locating objects, bats send out sound waves and listen for the echo to bounce off things.

6 MORE BAT MYTHS BUSTED!

ALL OF THE FOLLOWING STATEMENTS ARE UNTRUE. READ UP ON BATS TO FIND OUT MORE!

1 ALL BATS HAVE RABIES.

2 BATS FLY TOWARD AND GET TANGLED IN PEOPLE'S HAIR.

3 BATS SUCK PEOPLE'S BLOOD.

4 BATS ARE DIRTY.

5 BATS ARE RODENTS.

6 BATS ARE VAMPIRES IN DISGUISE.

MYTH

LIGHTNING NEVER STRIKES THE SAME PLACE TWICE.

ORIGIN

The myth is often traced to the 1860 book *Thrilling Adventures of the Prisoner of the Border*, in which author P. Hamilton Myers wrote, "Lightning never strikes twice in the same place . . ."

BUSTED!

THE NATIONAL OCEANIC AND ATMOSPHERIC ADMINISTRATION REPORTS THAT LIGHTNING DOES INDEED STRIKE SOME PLACES TWICE. It could be that something about a site makes it more likely to be struck; for example, taller objects are more likely to be struck than shorter objects.

On November 14, 1969, the APOLLO 12 SPACE-CRAFT WAS STRUCK BY LIGHTNING not once but twice within the first minute of its launch from Cape Canaveral.

MYTH

HUMANS USE ONLY 10% OF THEIR BRAINS.

ORIGIN

This statement is sometimes attributed to Albert Einstein, but there's no official record of him ever saying such a thing. In 1936, the idea that people use only 10 percent of their "mental ability" was published in the popular book *How to Win Friends and Influence People*.

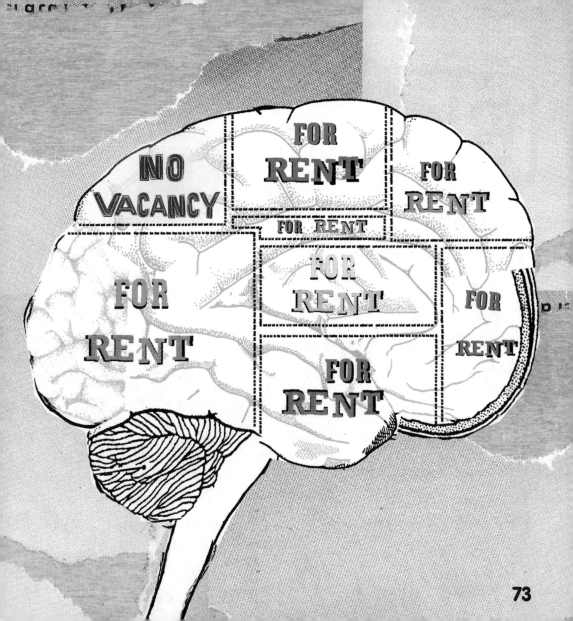

BUSTED!

THERE IS NO EVIDENCE THAT HUMANS USE ONLY 10% OF THEIR BRAINS.

In fact, scientists say, a person uses all of his or her brain. There are studies that show 100 percent of the brain's regions are active.

A 2009 study found that PLAYING THE VIDEO GAME *TETRIS* can change the brain. Several regions of the brain grew bigger in adolescent girls who played *Tetris* over three months.

MYTH

SHARKS KILL HUNDREDS OF PEOPLE A YEAR.

ORIGIN

Scary movies like *Jaws* and chilling news coverage of shark attacks fuel an illogical fear of being killed by the fish.

BUSTED!

SHARKS KILL NOWHERE NEAR HUNDREDS OF PEOPLE EACH YEAR; THEY DON'T EVEN KILL THAT MANY PEOPLE IN A DECADE. According to the International Shark Attack File, sharks killed 66 people worldwide between 2000 and 2011. The year 2011 saw the most deaths by shark, 12. In 2007, only one person was killed by a shark.

A shark can shed
THOUSANDS OF TEETH
over its lifetime.

10 THINGS MORE LIKELY TO KILL YOU THAN A SHARK

BEES, WASPS, AND HORNETS

TORNADOES

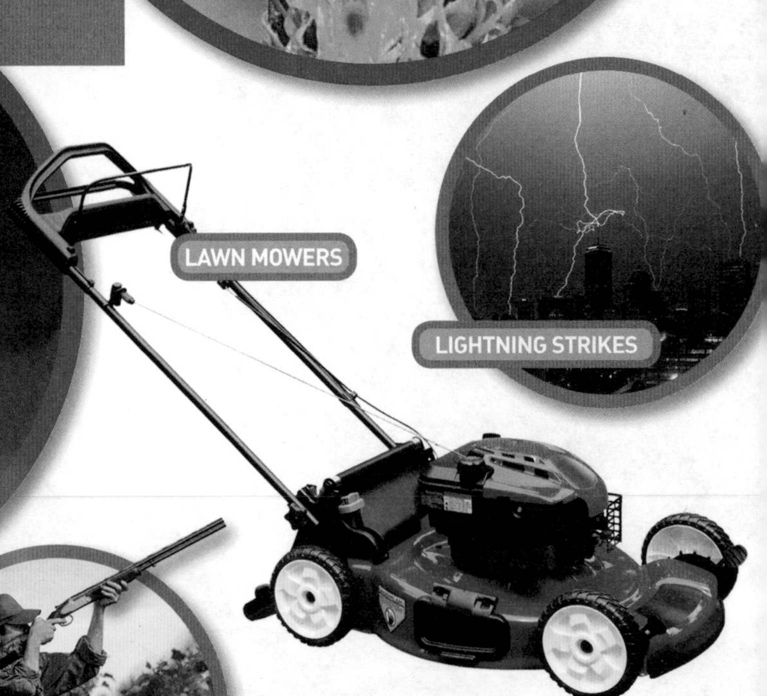

LAWN MOWERS

LIGHTNING STRIKES

HUNTING

TREE CLIMBING

VENOMOUS SNAKES

DOGS

EARTHQUAKES

FIREWORKS

81

MYTH

A FULL MOON MAKES PEOPLE ACT CRAZY.

ORIGIN

For thousands of years, scholars speculated that because the phases of the moon affect ocean tides, the water in a person's brain could be affected as well, leading to changes in behavior.

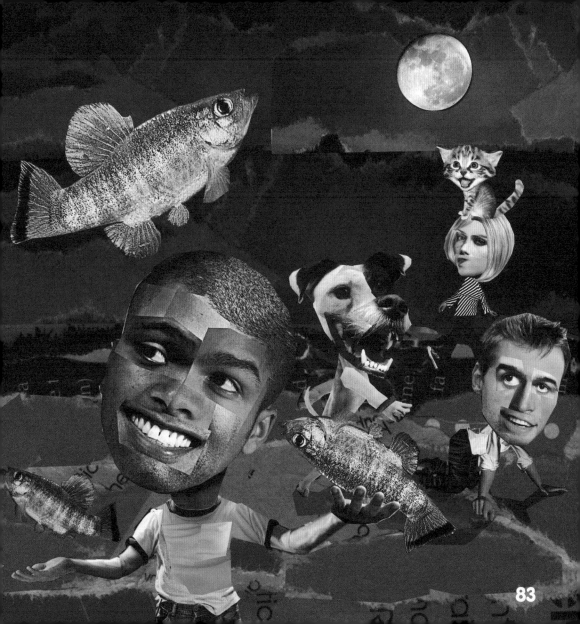

BUSTED!

THE MOON'S PHASES DON'T INFLUENCE THE WATER IN THE HUMAN BRAIN AND BODY. Multiple

studies have failed to find a
connection between a full moon and
things ranging from odd behavior
to traffic accidents to crime. Some
scientists speculate, however, that
because some mental disorders are
triggered by a lack of sleep, it's
possible that bright, full-moon
nights could lead to behavioral
changes in sleepless people with
such conditions.

The moon isn't round, but rather EGG-SHAPED, with the larger end pointed toward Earth.

MYTH

GEORGE WASHINGTON HAD

WOODEN TEETH.

ORIGIN

Dr. Scott Swank, curator of the National Museum of Dentistry, speculates the myth could have started for two reasons. The former U.S. President wore dentures made from ivory, the mammalian tusk material. Dark beverages such as coffee and tea, which Washington drank, can stain ivory over time, giving it an appearance similar to wood. Then, decades after Washington's death, a newspaper article reported his dentures scarcely resembled teeth and that the former President had a "wooden"

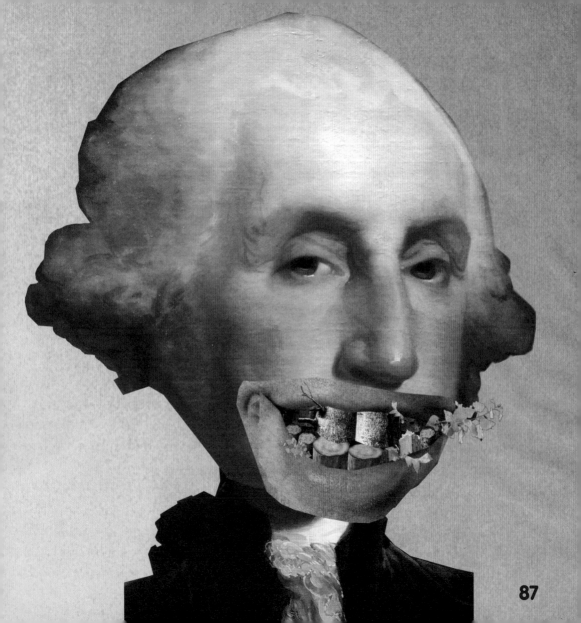

BUSTED!

SEVERAL DENTURES WORN BY WASHINGTON ARE STILL AROUND FOR SCIENTISTS AND DENTISTS TO STUDY.

In addition to ivory, the teeth of Washington's 18th-century dentures were made from human teeth, bovine teeth, and a very hard nut. The only appearance that wood makes is as small pegs attaching ivory teeth to the lower portion of one set of the President's dentures.

George Washington lost his first adult tooth when he was 22 YEARS OLD. By the time he was sworn in as President, at age 57, he had lost all but one tooth.

5 MORE WEIRD FACTS

ABOUT PRESIDENTIAL BODIES

TWO YEARS INTO HIS PRESIDENCY, JIMMY CARTER STARTED PARTING HIS HAIR ON THE LEFT, INSTEAD OF THE RIGHT.

GROVER CLEVELAND HAD A RUBBER JAW.

JAMES MADISON, ELECTED IN 1808, WAS THE FIRST PRESIDENT TO WEAR LONG PANTS INSTEAD OF KNEE BREECHES.

ABRAHAM LINCOLN WAS THE FIRST PRESIDENT TO SPORT A BEARD.

THEODORE ROOSEVELT LOST THE SIGHT IN HIS LEFT EYE AFTER BOXING INSIDE THE WHITE HOUSE.

MYTH

WATER DRAINS
ONE DIRECTION IN THE NORTHERN HEMISPHERE, THE OPPOSITE IN THE SOUTHERN HEMISPHERE.

ORIGIN
Confusion over a force called the Coriolis effect is behind this toilet-tested myth.

BUSTED!

THE CORIOLIS EFFECT, CAUSED BY EARTH'S ROTATION, dictates the direction that hurricanes spin: counterclockwise in the Northern Hemisphere, clockwise in the Southern Hemisphere. But the force is too small to act on water in toilets, bathtubs, and kitchen sinks; fluids there drain in both directions in both hemispheres. Other factors, such as the way water fills a sink or tub, also play a role in the direction water drains.

NO HURRICANES form at the Equator; the Coriolis effect there is too weak.

CATS ALWAYS LAND ON THEIR FEET UNHARMED.

ORIGIN

People have long been fascinated by a cat's ability to land on its feet after a fall. A French scientist in the late 1800s photographed a cat being dropped onto a bed to study how the animal moved midair into a feet-first position. As for a cat's feat to fall without injury: For thousands of years, people have associated the pets with mystical traits, such as having nine lives.

BUSTED!

"THE MYTH IS PROBABLY AT LEAST IN PART TRUE,"

says New York City, U.S.A., veterinarian Ann Hohenhaus. "The part that's true is that cats frequently appear to land on their feet. Veterinarians have studied cats that accidentally fell from windows, and the types of injuries— to the limbs, face, and chest—make them think that cats try really hard to and do land mostly on their feet." The part of the myth that's untrue, unfortunately, is that cats are invincible: In reality, cats don't always survive a fall.

Cats generally have FIVE TOES on their front paws, four on the back. But Jake the ginger tabby cat holds the record for the most toes: 28.

MYTH

YOUR HEART STOPS WHEN YOU SNEEZE.

ORIGIN

A change in pressure in the chest can cause the heart to adjust its rhythm, or beat, during a sneeze. That sensation—of "skipping a beat"—can seem like a heart-stopper.

BUSTED!

THE HEART DOESN'T STOP BEATING DURING A SNEEZE.
If anything, it just has a brief, slight change of pace. Think of it as the difference between a song ending and a song slowing down for a moment. Also, fluctuations in heartbeat are normal; even breathing in and breathing out cause slight changes.

A YouTube video of a BABY PANDA SNEEZING and startling its nearby mother has been viewed more than 138 million times.

99

MYTH

EATING POP ROCKS CANDY WHILE DRINKING SODA WILL KILL YOU.

ORIGIN

A rumor started that a popular character on a cereal commercial had died after eating Pop Rocks and drinking soda. Although it wasn't true, people kept talking about it. The U.S. Food and Drug Administration (FDA) opened a hotline to reassure parents that their children wouldn't be harmed.

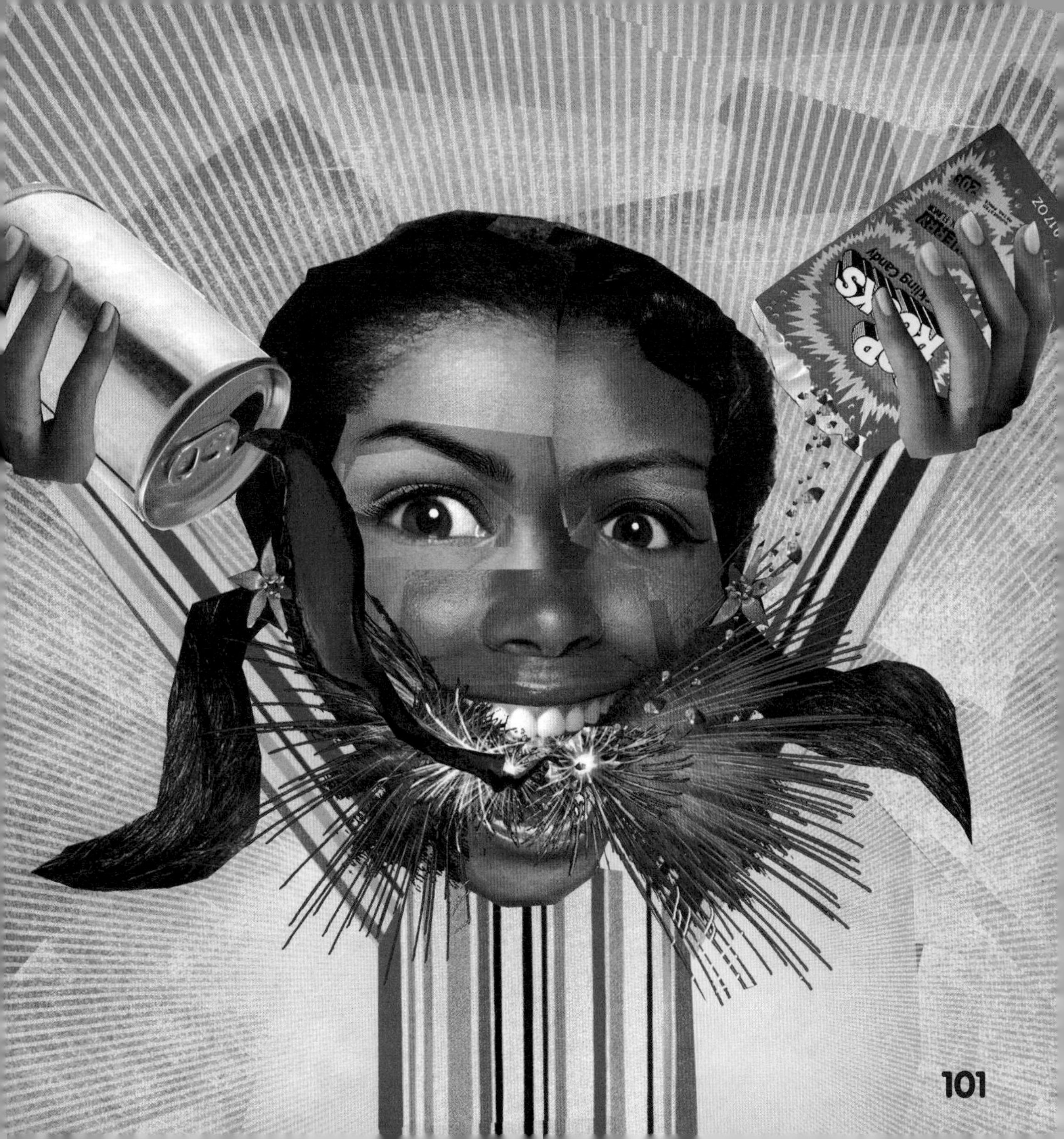

BUSTED!

PEOPLE FREAKED WHEN THEY THOUGHT THE GAS FROM ALL THAT CARBONATION WOULD CAUSE THEIR BELLIES TO EXPLODE.

In reality, carbon dioxide, which causes the gas, is so harmless that the FDA doesn't limit it in food. In fact, a package of Pop Rocks and a can of soda produce less gas than two sodas. But they do produce one big burp!

The food chemist who INVENTED POP ROCKS DID SO ACCIDENTALLY. He was trying to invent an instant soda. It didn't work, but Pop Rocks were born.

MYTH

TURKEY MAKES YOU SLEEPY BECAUSE IT CONTAINS A LOT OF TRYPTOPHAN.

ORIGIN

Many people report feeling tired after a Thanksgiving turkey dinner.
The bird often gets blamed for the drowsiness because it contains
tryptophan, which the body uses to produce a chemical that helps
regulate sleep.

BUSTED!

LIKE ALL PROTEIN, TURKEY CONTAINS TRYPTOPHAN.

But there's nothing exceptional about the amount of tryptophan in turkey. A chicken breast, cheesesteak sandwich, pork chop, and soybeans contain equal or greater amounts of tryptophan. Traveling, lots of socializing, and overeating are the likely culprits of post–Thanksgiving dinner drowsiness.

Ben Franklin wrote in a 1784 letter to his daughter that the turkey should replace the BALD EAGLE as the national bird of the United States. Franklin described the turkey as "though a little vain and silly, a bird of courage."

MYTH

IF A BIRD EATS RICE, ITS STOMACH WILL EXPLODE.

ORIGIN

Because dry rice expands when cooked, people probably thought a bird's stomach would expand with it. A more likely reason for this myth was to stop wedding guests from throwing rice, which makes the ground slippery for humans and can even get lodged in a person's ear.

BUSTED!

"A BIRD'S STOMACH DOESN'T REACH THE BOILING POINT NECESSARY FOR RICE TO EXPAND," says Erin Estell of the National Aviary. So the rice would never get to a harmful size. Plus, if this myth were true, there would be a lot fewer birds in the world. Many migrate through rice fields and feed on the rice!

Seagulls sometimes SIT ON PELICANS' HEADS and try to steal fish when the pelicans open their bills to empty out water.

MYTH

HAIR AND NAILS
CONTINUE TO GROW AFTER DEATH.

ORIGIN

The morbid myth has been around a long time but was popularized in the best-selling 1929 book *All Quiet on the Western Front*, in which the narrator imagines a dead friend's nails and hair growing.

BUSTED!

LOOKS CAN BE DECEIVING. After death,
skin dries out. As flesh loses water,
it shrinks, pulling away from hair
and nails and giving them the un-
settling appearance of lengthening.
But they aren't actually growing.
Nothing grows after death.

The **LONGEST BEARD** on a living man measures 8 feet 2.5 inches (2.5 m); the longest beard on a living woman is a mere 10.04 inches (25.5 cm).

THE GREAT WALL OF CHINA IS THE ONLY HUMAN-MADE OBJECT VISIBLE FROM SPACE.

ORIGIN

This far-out fable appeared in several publications in the late 19th century, including an 1895 book that claimed of the wall: "Besides its age it enjoys the reputation of being the only work of human hands on the globe visible from the moon."

BUSTED!

THERE ARE MANY HUMAN-MADE THINGS ON EARTH THAT AN ORBITING ASTRONAUT OR SATELLITE CAN SEE, though none are visible from as far away as the moon. Actually, it's quite difficult to see the wall from space, because the materials used to build it blend in with the surrounding land.

Though the Great Wall of China often is thought of as a **SINGLE WALL**, it was created in 220 B.C. by linking several different walls built during previous centuries.

6 HUMAN-MADE THINGS YOU CAN SEE FROM SPACE

THE ANCIENT PYRAMIDS AT GIZA

CITIES, ESPECIALLY AT NIGHT

LARGE DAMS AND RESERVOIRS

MAJOR HIGHWAYS

THE 2010 OIL SPILL IN THE GULF OF MEXICO

LARGE AIRPORTS

A PENNY DROPPED FROM THE EMPIRE STATE BUILDING COULD KILL SOMEONE BELOW.

ORIGIN

The urban legend has been around almost as long as the 1,250-foot-tall (381-m) building, which opened in New York City, U.S.A., in 1931.

BUSTED!

A PENNY FLUNG FROM THE ICONIC SKYSCRAPER COULDN'T KILL SOMEONE.

The coin is too flat and light; collisions with air molecules would slow it down to a nonlethal speed. But a ballpoint pen tossed off of a very tall building is a different story. Its streamlined shape could act as an arrow, piercing people at a speed of more than 200 miles per hour (321.9 km/h).

Every year, 73 ELEVATORS shuttle four million visitors to the Empire State Building's two observatories on the 86th and 102nd floors.

123

MYTH

NAPOLEON
WAS SHORT.

ORIGIN

Napoleon Bonaparte, the famous military leader and emperor of France in the early 1800s, was referred to as short even while alive. In fact, one of his nicknames was "Le Petit Caporal," or "the Little Corporal."

BUSTED!

ACCORDING TO RECORDS, NAPOLEON WAS LIKELY SOMEWHERE BETWEEN 5 FEET 6 INCHES (1.68 M) AND 5 FEET 7 INCHES (1.7 M) TALL. Professor Richard Steckel, who has spent years researching human height through history, says, "Frenchmen born in the late 1700s were about 5 feet 4 inches to 5 feet 5 inches (1.63 to 1.65 m) on average." So, in fact, Napoleon was taller than average!

Today, the average height of a U.S. male age 20 or older IS 5 FEET 9 INCHES (1.76 M) ; the average height of a U.S. woman in the same age range IS 5 FEET 3 INCHES (1.62 M).

125

MYTH

YOU SHOULD TILT YOUR HEAD BACK DURING A NOSEBLEED.

ORIGIN
Many people make the motion to avoid making a bloody mess.

126

BUSTED!

TILTING YOUR HEAD BACK IS THE EXACT OPPOSITE OF WHAT DOCTORS ADVISE.

A nosebleeder should tilt his or her head *forward* while standing or sitting, pinch the nostrils shut for ten minutes, and breathe through the mouth. Tilting the head back can send blood into the throat, which could cause vomiting.

EPISTAXIS is another word for nosebleed.

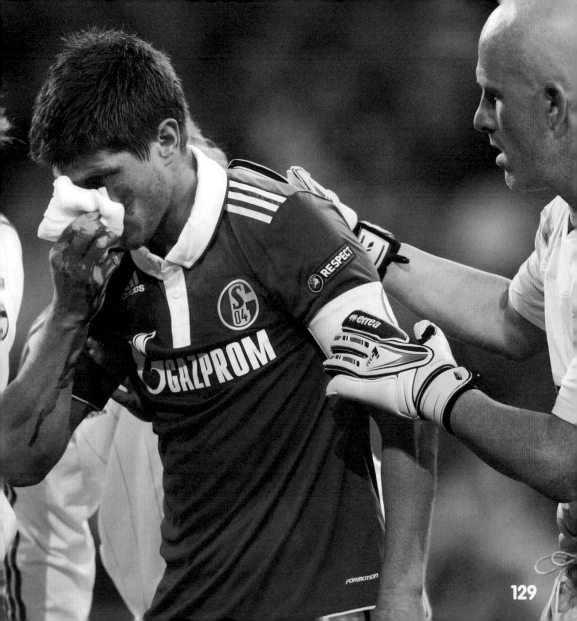

MYTH

SITTING TOO CLOSE
TO THE TV WILL MAKE YOU GO BLIND.

ORIGIN

Some older televisions emitted harmful rays
in amounts that exceed federal safety guidelines
in the United States.

130

BUSTED!

THERE IS NO SCIENTIFIC EVIDENCE THAT MODERN TELEVISIONS RELEASE RAYS THAT ARE HARMFUL TO THE EYES. Still, it's a good idea to move back: Sitting too close to the screen can cause eyestrain, an uncomfortable (but temporary) condition.

In February 2012, two fans of *THE SIMPSONS* set the world record for continuous TV-watching when they viewed 239 consecutive episodes of the animated series over 86 hours and 37 minutes.

6 MORE SIGHT MYTHS BUSTED!

ALL OF THE FOLLOWING STATEMENTS ARE UNTRUE.

1 READING IN DIM LIGHT WILL HURT YOUR EYES.

2 WEARING EYE-GLASSES TOO MUCH CAN MAKE EYES "WEAKER."

3 IF YOU SNEEZE WITH YOUR EYES OPEN, YOUR EYEBALLS WILL POP OUT.

4 FLUORESCENT LIGHT DAMAGES EYES.

5 DOGS AND CATS CAN'T SEE COLORS.

6 ALL SPIDERS HAVE EIGHT EYES.

ALLIGATORS LIVE IN THE SEWERS OF NEW YORK CITY, U.S.A.

ORIGIN

The scary story stems from a 1935 *New York Times* article in which teenagers reported pulling a live, 125-pound (56.7-kg) alligator out of a city sewer.

BUSTED!

It's illegal to keep an alligator as a pet in NEW YORK CITY, U.S.A.

WHEN ALLIGATORS ARE COLD, THEIR BODIES GO INTO SLOW MOTION.

"They need to sun themselves to give them energy," says herpetologist John L. Behler of New York City's Bronx Zoo, U.S.A. That means underground gators wouldn't have the strength to snap their jaws on prey or even digest what they could catch. Also, during storms, alligators would drown. "The sewers fill to the tippy-top," says Ian Michaels of the New York City Department of Environmental Protection.

6 ANIMALS THAT DO LIVE IN THE SEWERS OF NEW YORK CITY

RATS

BATS

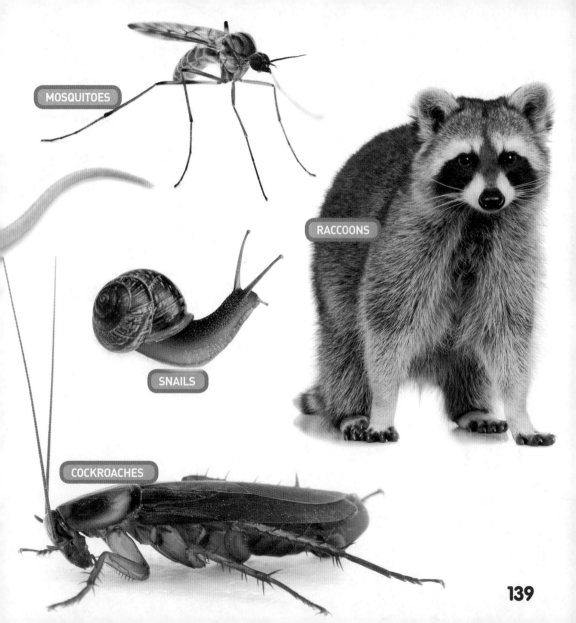

MOSQUITOES

RACCOONS

SNAILS

COCKROACHES

139

MYTH

TOUCHING A FROG OR TOAD WILL GIVE YOU WARTS.

warning contains **big wart**

ORIGIN

Many frogs and toads have bumps on their skin that look like warts. Some people think the bumps are contagious.

BUSTED!

"WARTS ARE CAUSED BY A HUMAN VIRUS, NOT FROGS OR TOADS,"

says dermatologist Jerry Litt. But the wartlike bumps behind a toad's ears *can* be dangerous. There, parotoid glands contain a nasty poison that irritates the mouths of some predators and often the skin of humans. So toads may not cause warts, but they can cause other nasties. It's best not to handle these critters—warts and all!

The golden poison dart frog is the deadliest frog in the world. A single frog measuring two inches (5 cm) has enough venom to kill ten grown men.

MYTH

BIGFOOT—
A CREATURE RESEMBLING A TALL, APELIKE PERSON— STALKS THE NORTH AMERICAN WILDERNESS.

ORIGIN

"The origin of the myth is impossible to pinpoint," says *Bigfoot Exposed* author and University of Florida anthropologist David Daegling. He notes that the beast became part of popular culture in 1958 when photographs of big footprints said to belong to Bigfoot were published in a northern California newspaper.

BUSTED!

THE VAST MAJORITY OF SCIENTISTS AGREE THAT THERE ISN'T SCIENTIFIC EVIDENCE TO SUPPORT THE EXISTENCE OF BIGFOOT. Most believe the legend is a hoax. "There are no bones at all, no teeth, and no hair or other material that can't be reasonably attributed to other known species," explains Daegling. "The things that would end the debate—bodies or bones—have *never* been found. We have to ask ourselves whether it's reasonable that an animal eight feet [2.4 m] tall has never been found after over fifty years of looking for it."

Many BIGFOOT BELIEVERS point to a 1967 short film shot in northern California that shows what appears to be a large, apelike creature walking on two legs through the woods.

10 MORE CREATURES THAT MOST LIKELY DON'T EXIST

UNICORN

DRAGON

MERMAID

CENTAUR

VAMPIRE

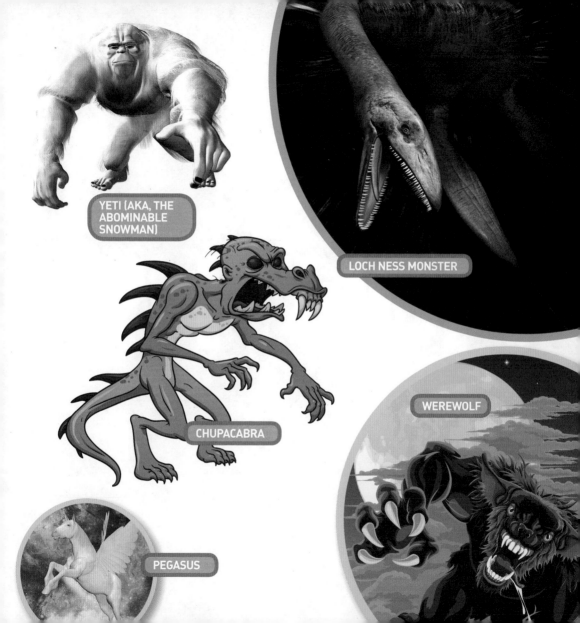

YETI (AKA, THE ABOMINABLE SNOWMAN)

LOCH NESS MONSTER

CHUPACABRA

WEREWOLF

PEGASUS

DOGS' MOUTHS ARE CLEANER THAN HUMANS'.

ORIGIN

Bite wounds from humans are more likely to become infected than those from dogs, according to some research. In addition, a dog's habit of licking its wounds can give the impression that it has super-clean saliva.

DOGS' MOUTHS AREN'T NECESSARILY ANY CLEANER THAN HUMANS', SCIENTISTS SAY.

Additional investigations on the subject by teenage science students have produced mixed results. One experiment found that dogs' mouths were dirtier; another found that human mouths were home to more bacteria. These experiments aren't very helpful anyway because comparing the germs found in a dog's mouth to those found in a person's is like comparing apples to oranges—most of the bacteria are species-specific—so you can't accurately measure the differences.

A normal human body is home to more than 10,000 SPECIES OF BACTERIA.

MYTH

IT'S BAD LUCK TO LET A BLACK CAT CROSS YOUR PATH.

ORIGIN

During medieval times—the period between the 5th and 15th centuries—many Europeans believed witches could turn into black cats.

153

BUSTED!

THE COLOR OF A CAT CAN'T CAUSE BAD LUCK.

In fact, a black cat's color may bring it *good* luck. Some scientists think the same gene that turns a cat's fur black might help it fight infections. Ancient Egyptians believed cats of *all* colors were lucky. "Cats were considered sacred," says Egyptologist Lorelei Corcoran. When a cat died in some Egyptian households, everyone shaved their eyebrows in mourning.

There are about 130,000 HAIRS PER SQUARE INCH on a cat's belly.

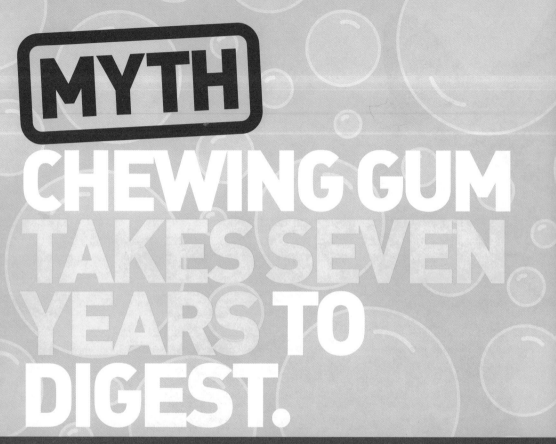

MYTH

CHEWING GUM TAKES SEVEN YEARS TO DIGEST.

ORIGIN

It's unclear exactly where this bit of fiction began, but let's not forget that gum is rather sticky, and if you didn't know that most healthy people can move objects through the digestive tract quickly, you might think a wad of gum could get stuck there for quite a while.

BUSTED!

GUM IS MADE FROM A SUBSTANCE SIMILAR TO RUBBER,

so it's impossible for the acid in your stomach to break it down. But that doesn't mean the gum sticks around. It can't adhere to the slippery lining in your gut, so as long as you don't make meals out of it, gum will come out of your body with the rest of your waste. "In a couple days, it comes out looking pretty much the same as when it went in," says David E. Milov, a doctor at Nemours Children's Hospital in Orlando, Florida, U.S.A.

Humans have chewed gum in one form or another FOR THOUSANDS OF YEARS. In the Stone Age, people CHEWED TREE BARK.

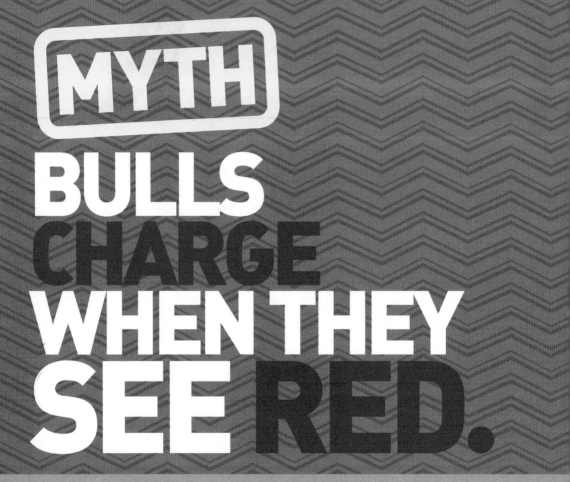

MYTH

BULLS CHARGE WHEN THEY SEE RED.

ORIGIN

Traditionally, a red cape is part of a bullfighter's colorful costume. When the bullfighter flashes the cape at the bull, the bull charges.

BUSTED!

MOVEMENT ACTUALLY MAKES A BULL CHARGE. "I've seen bulls chase everything from red to blue to plaid," says Temple Grandin of Colorado State University. "It's the motion of the bullfighter's cape, not the color."

A study showed that athletes who wear red uniforms have a BETTER CHANCE OF WINNING than athletes who wear other colors.

MOTHER BIRDS WILL REJECT THEIR BABIES IF THEY'VE BEEN TOUCHED BY HUMANS.

ORIGIN

Well-meaning humans who find a chick on the ground may want to return the baby bird to the nest. But the bird is probably learning to fly and shouldn't be disturbed. The tale may have been invented to keep people from handling young birds.

BUSTED!

"MOST BIRDS HAVE A POORLY DEVELOPED SENSE OF SMELL," says Michael Mace, bird curator at the San Diego Zoo's Wild Animal Park in California, U.S.A. "They won't notice a human scent." One exception: vultures, who sniff out dead animals for dinner. But you wouldn't want to mess with a vulture anyway!

They may not smell very well, but BIRDS HAVE EXCEPTIONAL VISION. Hawks can see eight times better than humans.

MYTH

OPOSSUMS HANG BY THEIR TAILS.

ORIGIN

Opossums use their tails to grasp branches as they climb trees. So it's not surprising that people believe they also use them to *hang* from branches.

BUSTED!

A BABY OPOSSUM CAN HANG FROM ITS TAIL FOR A FEW SECONDS, BUT AN ADULT IS TOO HEAVY. Besides, says Paula Arms of the National Opossum Society, that wouldn't help them survive. "Why would they just hang around? That skill isn't useful —there's no point."

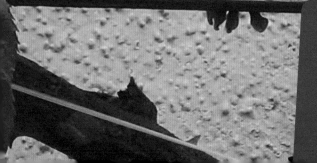

When frightened or startled, opossums will **CURL UP WITH THEIR TONGUE OUT** and play dead for several minutes, or up to a few hours!

10 OTHER ANIMALS THAT HANG AROUND IN TREES

CLOUDED LEOPARDS

BATS

KINKAJOUS

BIRDS

ORANGUTANS

GORILLAS

KOALAS

SNAKES

CHIMPANZEES

LEMURS

173

MYTH

PENGUINS
FALL BACKWARD
WHEN THEY
LOOK UP AT
AIRPLANES.

ORIGIN
Legend has it that British pilots buzzing around islands off South America saw penguins toppling over like dominoes when the birds looked skyward.

BUSTED!

AN EXPERIMENT TESTING THE STORY FOUND THAT PENGUINS

are perfectly capable of maintaining their footing, even if they're watching airplanes. "But the reality isn't funny," says John Shears, who worked on the survey. "Low-flying aircraft can cause penguins to panic and leave their nests."

An AFRICAN BLACK-FOOTED PENGUIN can swim at 15 miles per hour (24 km/h), but on land it WADDLES AT 2 MILES PER HOUR (3.2 km/h).

175

MYTH
ELEPHANTS ARE AFRAID OF MICE.

ORIGIN
People used to think that mice liked to crawl into elephants' trunks. "They thought that would cause great damage and terrible sneezing," says Jack Hanna of the Columbus Zoo in Ohio, U.S.A. So it makes sense that elephants would be afraid of the rodents.

BUSTED!

ALTHOUGH ELEPHANTS DO GET ANXIOUS WHEN THEY HEAR PITTER-PATTERING sounds they can't identify, an elephant's eyesight is so poor that it could barely even see a mouse. Plus, if an elephant isn't afraid to live among predators such as tigers, rhinos, and crocodiles, a mouse would be the least of its worries!

An ELEPHANT'S TRUNK has more muscles than you have in your body!

MYTH

IT'S BAD LUCK TO OPEN AN UMBRELLA INDOORS.

ORIGIN

Asians in ancient times believed in gods of the skies. Royalty often used umbrellas to shield themselves from sunlight. Opening an umbrella where the sun's rays didn't fall could have been interpreted as offensive to the sun.

BUSTED!

OPENING AN UMBRELLA IN YOUR LIVING ROOM MAY CAUSE YOU TO BREAK A LAMP OR TWO, BUT IT WON'T BRING BAD LUCK. Opening it under clear skies, though, can definitely be lucky. When your skin is exposed to sun, ultraviolet rays can cause damage like sunburn. So protecting your skin—whether it's with sunscreen or an umbrella—is always a good idea.

The artists **CHRISTO AND JEANNE-CLAUDE** exhibited 3,100 yellow and blue umbrellas—all more than 19 feet (5.8 m) tall—in valleys in California, U.S.A., and Japan.

MYTH

GOLDFISH HAVE ONLY A THREE-SECOND MEMORY.

ORIGIN

An adult human's brain weighs about three pounds (1.36 kg), whereas an average goldfish's brain weighs only a tiny fraction of that. So how could there be any room for memory in there?

BUSTED!

RESEARCH HAS SHOWN THAT GOLDFISH ARE QUITE SMART. Phil Gee of the University of Plymouth in the United Kingdom trained goldfish to push a lever that dropped food into their tank. "They remembered the time of day that the lever worked and waited until feeding time to press it," Gee says. One scientist even trained goldfish to tell the difference between classical and blues music!

142 BILLION GOLDFISH crackers are made every year.

MYTH

A CAMEL'S HUMP HOLDS WATER.

ORIGIN

Thousands of years ago, desert nomads probably noticed how far a camel could travel without water. They might have assumed its hump stored extra H_2O.

BUSTED!

FEW ANIMALS CAN LAST A WEEK WITHOUT WATER, but a camel can survive up to two weeks. One reason is that a camel can get extra moisture it needs from fat—and that's what is stored in its hump. "The hump is composed of up to 80 pounds (36.3 kg) of fat for nourishment," says Jack Hanna of the Columbus Zoo in Ohio, U.S.A.

One of the SOUNDS USED TO MAKE CHEWBACCA'S VOICE in the *Star Wars* movies was made by a camel!

MYTH

FORTUNE COOKIES COME FROM CHINA.

ORIGIN

Fortune cookies were invented in Japan and then made their appearance in Japanese restaurants in the United States in the early 1900s. American Chinese restaurants started regularly serving the cookies after World War II.

BUSTED!

FORTUNE COOKIES AREN'T EVEN FOUND IN CHINA!

"They most likely came from Japan," says Jennifer 8. Lee, author of *The Fortune Cookie Chronicles*. The proof: an 1878 Japanese book that shows a man baking fortune cookies. Chinese people weren't associated with the treats until at least 1907. "The cookies were brought to California, U.S.A., by Japanese immigrants," Lee says. It's still a mystery why fortune cookies are now served mostly in Chinese restaurants.

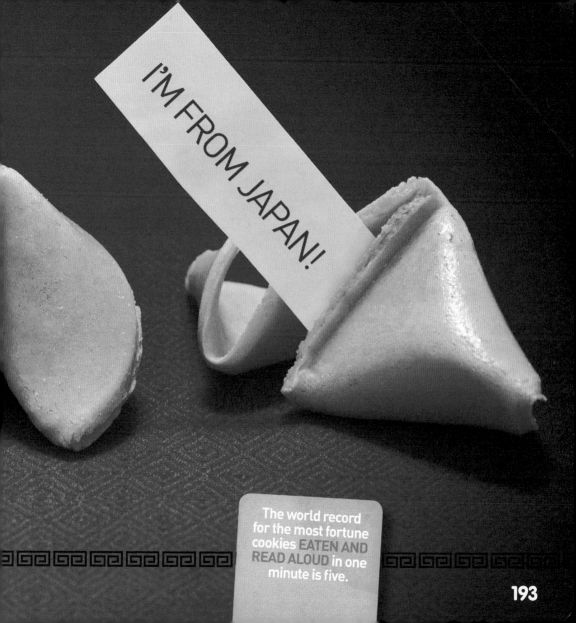

I'M FROM JAPAN!

The world record for the most fortune cookies EATEN AND READ ALOUD in one minute is five.

8 MORE THINGS THAT DIDN'T COME FROM WHERE YOU THINK THEY DID

DANISH (PASTRY)
MYTH: DENMARK
BUSTED! AUSTRIA

KIWIFRUIT
MYTH: NEW ZEALAND
BUSTED! CHINA

CHEWING GUM
MYTH: U.S.A.
BUSTED! ANCIENT GREECE

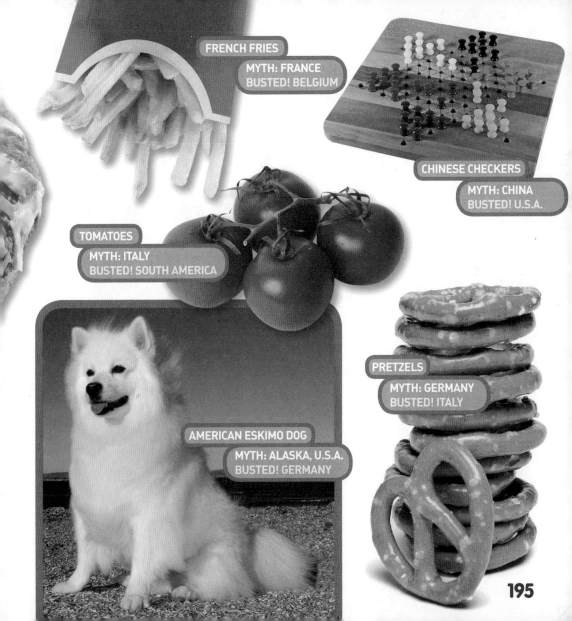

FRENCH FRIES
MYTH: FRANCE
BUSTED! BELGIUM

CHINESE CHECKERS
MYTH: CHINA
BUSTED! U.S.A.

TOMATOES
MYTH: ITALY
BUSTED! SOUTH AMERICA

PRETZELS
MYTH: GERMANY
BUSTED! ITALY

AMERICAN ESKIMO DOG
MYTH: ALASKA, U.S.A.
BUSTED! GERMANY

MYTH

TAPPING THE TOP OF A SODA CAN KEEPS IT FROM SPRAYING WHEN YOU OPEN IT.

ORIGIN

Even though tapping the top of a can does nothing, it certainly feels like you are helping. This one most likely spread through an endless web of word-of-mouth tips and hints.

BUSTED!

SODA IS FIZZY BECAUSE OF A GAS CALLED CARBON DIOXIDE (CO_2).

At the top of the can is a little extra CO_2 that's released with a harmless hiss when you open the soda. If you shake the can, that gas mixes with the soda, making it more bubbly and creating foam that sprays out. Many people think tapping the top of the can will burst the new bubbles and settle the foam. Recent studies show that while that does no good, there might be something to the theory of side-tapping, to release the bubbles from the side and bottom of the can. But really, the only surefire way to defizz the foam is to absorb it into the liquid. "That takes time, not tapping," says Joseph F. Dues of Purdue University in Indiana, U.S.A.

A Double Gulp soda cup holds MORE THAN FOUR CANS OF SODA in it (without ice).

MYTH

SPIRITS WILL HAUNT YOU IF YOU DON'T HOLD YOUR BREATH WHEN YOU PASS A GRAVEYARD.

ORIGIN

"People once believed that spirits of the dead could enter through the nose or mouth," says folklorist Elizabeth Tucker.

BUSTED!

There is an UNDERWATER CEMETERY off the coast of Miami, Florida, U.S.A., in the form of a man-made reef that includes sculptures and benches.

THE DEAD CAN'T ENTER THROUGH YOUR NOSE AND MOUTH.

Living things do, though almost all are harmless. "Kids inhale around 30,000 times a day," says pulmonologist Daniel Culver, an expert on the respiratory, or breathing, system. "Every day, you breathe in hundreds of millions of bacteria and fungi." Most won't hurt you. When dangerous bacteria *do* enter your lungs, your body is usually able to fight them off.

INDEX

INDEX

Published by the National Geographic Society

John M. Fahey, *Chairman of the Board and
   Chief Executive Officer*
Timothy T. Kelly, *President*
Declan Moore, *Executive Vice President;
   President, Publishing and Digital Media*
Melina Gerosa Bellows, *Executive Vice
   President; Chief Creative Officer, Books, Kids, and Family*

Prepared by the Book Division

Hector Sierra, *Senior Vice President and General Manager*
Nancy Laties Feresten, *Senior Vice President,
   Kids Publishing and Media*
Jonathan Halling, *Design Director, Books and
   Children's Publishing*
Jay Sumner, *Director of Photography, Children's Publishing*
Jennifer Emmett, *Vice President, Editorial
   Director, Children's Books*
Eva Absher-Schantz, *Design Director, Kids Publishing and Media*
Carl Mehler, *Director of Maps*
R. Gary Colbert, *Production Director*
Jennifer A. Thornton, *Director of Managing Editorial*

Staff for This Book

Becky Baines, *Project Editor*
Eva Absher-Schantz, *Art Director*
Lori Epstein, *Senior Illustrations Editor*
Kate Olesin, *Associate Editor*
Ariane Szu-Tu, *Editorial Assistant*
Kathryn Robbins, *Associate Designer*
Hillary Moloney, *Illustrations Assistant*
Stefan Lovgren, C. M., Tomlin, Jamie Kiffel-Alcheh,
   Contributing Writers
Grace Hill, *Associate Managing Editor*
Joan Gossett, *Production Editor*
Lewis R. Bassford, *Production Manager*
Susan Borke, *Legal and Business Affairs*

Manufacturing and Quality Management

Phillip L. Schlosser, *Senior Vice President*
Chris Brown, *Vice President, Book Manufacturing*
George Bounelis, *Vice President, Production Services*
Nicole Elliott, Rachel Faulise, Robert L. Barr, *Managers*

This book is dedicated to anyone who ever encouraged me
to tell the truth or made me laugh. Thank you. —EK

The National Geographic Society is one of the world's largest
nonprofit scientific and educational organizations. Founded
in 1888 to "increase and diffuse geographic knowledge," the
Society's mission is to inspire people to care about the planet.
It reaches more than 400 million people worldwide each
month through its official journal, *National Geographic*, and
other magazines; National Geographic Channel; television
documentaries; music; radio; films; books; DVDs; maps;
exhibitions; live events; school publishing programs; interactive
media; and merchandise. National Geographic has funded
more than 10,000 scientific research, conservation and explora-
tion projects and supports an education program promoting
geographic literacy.

For more information, please visit
www.nationalgeographic.com, call 1-800-NGS LINE (647-5463),
or write to the following address:
National Geographic Society
1145 17th Street N.W.
Washington, D.C. 20036-4688 U.S.A.

Visit us online at www.nationalgeographic.com/books

For librarians and teachers: www.ngchildrensbooks.org

More for kids from National Geographic:
kids.nationalgeographic.com

For information about special discounts for bulk purchases,
please contact National Geographic Books
Special Sales: ngspecsales@ngs.org

For rights or permissions inquiries, please contact National
Geographic Books Subsidiary Rights:
ngbookrights@ngs.org

Printed in Hong Kong
14/THK/2

ABOUT THE ART

"To make these crazy collages, I start with a line drawing and layer pieces of collage on top. Backgrounds can start as torn paper doodles and then become landscapes or interiors. It's amazing what you can make from a scrap of paper!"

—Tom Nick Cocotos

Check out the artist online!
www.cocotos.com

Library of Congress Cataloging-in-Publication Data
Krieger, Emily.
  Myths busted! : just when you thought you knew what you knew-- / by Emily Krieger ; illustrated by Tom Nick Cocotos.
    p. cm.
  Includes index.
  ISBN 978-1-4263-1102-4 (pbk. : alk. paper) -- ISBN 978-1-4263-1103-1 (library edition : alk. paper)
  1. Common fallacies--Juvenile literature. I. Cocotos, Tom Nick, ill. II. Title.
  AZ999.K75 2013
  001.9'6--dc23

                        2012039323